Virtual Book Tours

Effective Online Book Promotion From the Comfort of Your Own Home

I0426579

By Jo Linsdell

First Printing: 2013
ISBN - 13-978-1492920939
ISBN - 10-149292032

www.JoLinsdell.com

About the Author

"Jo is one of those rare writers who really "gets" not only the art of writing but the business and promotional sides as well. In addition to her books and e-books, she's done a great service for the writing community through her Promo Day efforts, and anyone taking her on in a writing or editorial capacity would certainly benefit from her practical knowledge and experience in that area."

Jennifer Mattern, *Owner, JH Mattern Communications*

Jo Linsdell is the author of five books, including *Italian for Tourists, A Guide to Weddings in Italy, Out and About at the Zoo,* and *Fairy May*, as well as being the illustrator of the *A Birthday Clown for Archer* series (written by Kathy Mashburn). She is also the founder of Writers and Authors and Promo Day. Linsdell studied A-levels in Business Studies, History and Art and has won several awards in her career. She was named the *Who's Who in the writing industry* in 2009.

Contents

Preface

"Nobody ever made money writing a book- only by selling it"

Brian Jud

In April 2013 Eric Schmit, Executive chairman at Google, stated in a post on Google+ that "nearly everyone will be online by 2020". Whilst you might automatically scoff at this bold statement, given that 2020 is now less 7 years away, there may well be a high chance that his prediction comes true.

According to statistics on *World Internet Stats* over 34.3% of the worlds population was using the internet mid-year 2012. In countries like Africa and Latin America the number of internet users is growing at an amazing rate.

Then of course we have the rapidly increasing use of smart-phones, tablets and other mobile devices. Garter has said that "mobile phones will overtake PCs as the most common web access device worldwide by 2013" and that "the number of smart-phones will exceed 1.82 billion unities worldwide in 2013."

So what does all this mean for writers? It means that your target audience is online and just a click away. You can now reach your readers from the comfort of your own home and successfully promote your books to a global audience at little or no cost.

A book tour has long been known as one of the most effective ways of creating a buzz about your book and growing your author brand. With internet you now have the opportunity to do a virtual book tour and reach even more people whilst leaving a virtual footprint that will keep your marketing efforts working for you long after the event is over.

As soon as I heard about virtual book tours I was sold on the idea. It was the perfect solution for me. I'm from the UK and write predominately in English but live in Italy. My target readers are in other countries and so being able to reach them through the internet has, to a large extent, made my writing career possible. I doubt I would have sold many books without it.

I've done many virtual book tours and with each one I learn something new. My goal is that **Virtual Book Tours: Effective Online Book Promotion From the Comfort of Your Own Home** will help you to be able to organize and carry out a successful virtual book tour of your own and in doing so contribute to the success of your books.

Section 1: What is a Virtual Book Tour?

What is a Virtual Book Tour: Chapter 1

What are Virtual Book Tours?

"Don't be afraid to get creative and experiment with your marketing."

Mike Volpe

Virtual Book Tours

Book promotion has changed a lot over the years and the introduction of the internet, and with it blogs, started a revolution in how authors can reach their target audience and connect with their readers.

In the past authors would do book signings, readings, radio and television interviews, and aim at book reviews from noted publications in a hope of spreading the word about their books.

Whilst these methods are still valid in today's market they are limited. For a start, organising such promotions is difficult especially for new authors and even more so for those self publishing. It's true the reputation of self publishing has changed immensely in recent years and it no longer has the same stigma attached to it... that said some of the larger bookstore chains and publications still prefer to work with agents and well known traditional Publishers.

This is just one of the many reasons why virtual book tours are such a great idea. Everyone can do one. No exceptions. With a little knowledge of social media and blogging you can easily set up a virtual book tour to promote your latest release or put new life into an older project.

So what is a virtual book tour? A virtual book tour is when you tour the web over a set period of time promoting your book. (I'll go into the different types of stops you can include in your tour later in chapter 3).

There are various ways you can set up your tour. Some authors choose to do a tour lasting anywhere from a week to a couple of months where they are hosted on different sites each day. Others prefer to do a tour that lasts for several months but only has one or two hosts per week.

Then there's the question of content. Some are review only tours where the only type of stops on the tour are for reviews of your book. Others include a large variety of stop types and use all kinds of media and technology during their tours.

All these elements come down to your goals for the tour, the type of content you feel most comfortable doing and the amount of time you have to work on your tour.

So why do a virtual book tour?

Reason 1: Sell more books

As with all book marketing the main aim is to sell more books. In order to sell more books people need to know your book exists. A virtual book tour is one of the most effective methods of sending your book viral and reaching a large audience. A virtual book tour will help you sell more books by:

- **Collecting reviews**. The best promotion a book can get is by word of mouth, which is one of the reasons why having your book reviewed can have a huge impact on number of sales. When the public reads how others are enjoying your book it increases their curiosity about it. Reviews are a powerful tool and can be used again and again meaning they have both an instant and longer term impact.

Obviously the more reviews you have on your product sales pages the better. This is where people actually decide whether or not to buy your book but having reviews posted to blogs is also beneficial. You can always add them to the book description section of you sales page as editorial reviews. (I'll be covering reviews in more detail in reason 3)

By having lots of reviews on your product page Amazon will list your book in their "Top Rated" lists giving you some valuable free publicity.

- **Create a buzz**. A virtual book tour is the perfect way to create a buzz about your book. When people see your book being mentioned across various websites, blogs and other channels it registers in their brain. The more they see it mentioned the more they remember it. The more people talking about it the bigger the buzz. It creates a snowball effect and sends your book viral.

- **Become a best seller**. A virtual book tour can help you become a best seller which in turn helps you sell yet more books. Best seller rankings are calculated over a small period of time (Amazon for example updates their lists hourly). One way to be able to claim best seller status is to reach it during a free download day. Whilst this won't gain you any royalties for copies downloaded during that period you will be able to use your success to increase the number of reviews your book has, create more buzz for your book and be able to take screenshots of your book in the top rankings. Hitting the best seller list will also kick start Amazon's algorithm and they will start pushing your book more to the public. A book that is successful on a free day will result as popular which will make Amazon highlight it more on site and suggest it in their email promotions too.

- **Connecting with readers**. Relationships matter. Readers like to know about the people writing books as well as about the books themselves. A virtual book tour is a great way to build relationships with your target audience and in doing so increase your chances of sales.

Reason 2: Build your author brand

As an author your brand is you. By doing a virtual book tour you build on your author brand and show that you are an expert in your field. A strong author brand equals more sales. Think about it. Which book would you buy? One by someone you've never heard of before or one by an author you've seen mentioned repeatedly and know a bit about? Almost definitely the latter. Even if a customer can't remember why they know your name the fact that it's familiar to them may be the push they need to make them buy your book instead of another.

Having a strong author brand usually has the knock on effect of having a more active fan base too. Your readers feel they know you better and give more value to your work. It creates an element of trust and makes them feel more comfortable buying your books as they know you're an expert in your field.

So how can you build your author brand through a virtual book tour?

- **Doing interviews**. In what ever format the interviews take place they will help build your author brand. They allow the public to get to know you as a person whilst at the same time showing your experience and highlighting your successes.

- **Writing guest posts.** One of the best ways to build your author brand is by writing guest posts for publication on other peoples websites and blogs.
- **Presenting webinars.** This clearly shows you are an expert in your niche and strengthens your author brand.

Reason 3: Collect reviews

The third reason is to collect reviews. As I mentioned before reviews are great for both immediate impact and long term marketing. Having others tell people about your book is a lot more effective than you telling everyone about it. It's also much more likely to lead to more sales. Word of mouth advertising is the best type of publicity your book can get and a review is just that. It's the honest opinion from someone who has read your book and holds more weight with potential buyers than anything else.

A Virtual Book Tour is perfect for collecting more reviews as you can send out copies in exchange for review on websites and blogs but also use your tour stops to encourage anyone buying the book to leave their own review. Sometimes all you need to do is ask.

Do You Have the Right Stuff?

Before we go any further you need to ask yourself if you have what it takes to organise a Do-It-Yourself virtual book tour.

You'll need to consider whether you're going to organize the tour yourself or use a virtual tour company service to set one up for you. This book is designed to give you all the information you need to set up your own tour but there are numerous tour companies out there that you can pay to find stops for you. This might be worth considering if; you're a new author and haven't yet built up a strong author brand, have no contacts, lack experience in blogging and being interviewed or just don't have the time to find your own stops.

Be warned though, not all tour companies have the same value. There's an increasing number of them appearing on the internet and from my own personal experience working as a host with numerous companies I can honestly tell you that some are amazing whilst others aren't worth a cent.

If you do choose to use a tour company make sure they are professional and well organized. Ask authors they have represented in the past if they were pleased with the results and do a search to find testimonials for their services.

Also make sure they are right for your genre and have experience in doing tours for books in your niche area. For example Partners in Crime tours are excellent for books in the crime and mystery genre whilst World of Ink do a great job for children's books.

Which ever route you take to creating your virtual book tour it will be good for visibility, strengthen your author brand and help create a buzz about your book.

What are Virtual Book Tours: Chapter 2

How do Virtual Book Tours work?

"I like to define networking as cultivating mutually beneficial, give-and-take, win-win relationships... The end result may be to develop a large and diverse group of people who will gladly and continually refer a lot of business to us, while we do the same for them."

Bob Burg

How do virtual book tours work?

This chapter provides an understanding of how virtual book tours work, but before we jump into the tour process it's important to mention a few key points:

- **Goals**: Know what your goals are for your tour. This is vital for the success of your tour. You may have more than one goal e.g. collect reviews, reach best seller status and sell over 1000 copies. Now that you know your goals and have clear objectives of what you want to achieve with your tour, you'll be able to focus on the content that will best help you realize your goals.

  For example, your goal is to collect reviews for your book. Your tour will therefore be centred around a review campaign. Your stops will be focused on reviews. You will target review sites and top Amazon reviewers in your genre to publish their review of your book. You might organize a free download day promoting it on various sites (we'll cover that in more detail in chapter 15) and encourage readers to leave a review. You might also decide to set up a give-away. Again the focus will be on encouraging winners to leave a review.

- **Metrics**: In order to measure the success of your tour you need to check your metrics before, during and after your tour period.

  Some of the statistics to check include:

  - Amazon Author Rank
  - Amazon Seller Rank

- Average sales per month (if putting new life into an older title so you can see the difference the tour makes to your usual results).
- Number of likes to your Facebook page
- Number of followers on Twitter
- Number of people that have you in circles on Google+
- Average page views on your blog
- Average hits to your website.

During your virtual book tour you'll want to make note of the stops that get the most interactions (comments and shares) and if possible get the page view statistics from your host so you can see which stops had the most social impact.

The Process of a virtual book tour

Now let's take a look at the process of a virtual book tour.

Setting the tour period

First you need to set your tour period. Will you be doing a week, month or longer? Will you do a post once a week, daily posts or multiple posts on the same days?

Some people choose to do just one stop a week but have the tour last several months. This type of tour tends to be low impact but is good for keeping your book current.

Alternatively you might want to do multiple stops on the same days during one week. This type of tour is often based around *book blasts* (when your book is featured in a spotlight post on as many sites as possible).

The most powerful and high impact tours tend to be those that last one to three months with a stop on every day. These tours often include various types of content.

Types of stops

As I mentioned before this will depend largely on the goals you've set for the virtual book tour. Some examples include guest posts, interviews, reviews and book spotlight features. (I'll discuss the various options more in chapter 3).

Target audience

If you want to maximize the impact of your virtual book tour you need to go where your target audience is. For example, a children's book author should look for stops on parenting blogs and target sites that specialize in reviewing children's books.

An author of a historical romance novel should look for stops on sites that specialize in romance or the time period in which the novel is set.

For this book my target audience is authors and so I would look for stops on sites that tailor to the writing and publishing industry. I'd look for blogs about book marketing and author branding.

You get the idea. It's about reaching the right people with your content. We'll go into this in more detail in chapter 4.

Schedule stops

Now you know; your goals, your tour period, the types of stops you want to include and the sort of sites to visit in order to reach your target audience. Next you need to schedule your tour stops.

I'll cover how to find tour stops in more detail in chapter 5 but basically you need to query hosts and sign them up to be part of your virtual book tour.

Give them all the information they need and explain exactly what you want from them and what you'll give them, being as brief and clear as possible. It's a good idea to attach your media kit so they have all the relevant information available.

Promote

You'll want to promote your tour as much as possible (see chapters 9 and 10 for more details regarding promotional materials and how to promote a tour).

Recycle content and share

One of the great things about a virtual book tour is that the stops can be used long after the tour is over. In chapter 11 we'll take a closer look at what happens post-tour.

What is a Virtual Book Tour: Chapter 3

Types of stops

"Accept what life offers you and try to drink from every cup. All wines should be tasted; some should only be sipped, but with others, drink the whole bottle."

Paulo Coelho

What kind of stops can you include in a virtual book tour?

Virtual book tours offer complete flexibility when it comes to the types of content that you can include. As I mentioned earlier, the types of stops you decide to include in your virtual book tour will depend on your goals. They will also be influenced by your strengths and weaknesses and your comfort zone.

When choosing the types of stops to include you should consider your skills. Do you excel in creating powerful video content? If you have no idea how to record a quality video it's probably best that you don't concentrate your tour on video content. Do you have a good working knowledge of social media? If not, maybe it would be best to cut out social chats. Do you have a very soft voice? If so, it may be best to avoid radio interviews.

Make a list of your strengths and weaknesses. Here's some ideas of the type of things to include:

- **Personality traits**. Are you a natural chatter box? Do you look good on film?

- **Skills**. Do you have a good working knowledge of social media sites? Can you create awesome presentations? Is your strong point writing articles? Or are you a video wizard?

- **Physical limits**. Soft voice, camera shy, etc...

- **Environmental obstacles**. Limited time available for live chats, don't own a webcam, etc...

Next think about your comfort zone. We all have one. It's that place we feel at ease. Stepping out of your comfort zone means trying something new and pushing yourself to overcome your fears.

Whilst I suggest concentrating the majority of your tour stops in your strength areas, a virtual book tour (especially a longer one) is a great opportunity to branch out and try something new. Never done a social chat before? Schedule one for experience during your tour. Not only will you learn a new skill but you'll also reach a different kind of audience than you do with your usual comfort zone content.

Now let's take a closer look at the different types of stops you can include;

Social chats. The power of social media sites is huge. According to a new eMarketer report, "Worldwide Social Network Users: 2013 Forecast and Comparative Estimates," nearly one in four people worldwide will use social networks in 2013. This makes them the perfect place for reaching out to your audience. Let's take a look at the different kinds of social chats you can do:

- **Facebook Wall Chats**. 1 out of 5 people on the internet uses Facebook. The total number of Facebook users now stands at over 1.15 billion and 699 million of them are daily users. A Facebook Wall Chat is basically a live written interview that takes place on the page of your host. Most of these question and answer sessions take place on the same thread so the chat can easily be followed and shared.

- **Live Twitter interviews**. The average number of tweets sent per day is 400 million and Twitter boasts over 200 million monthly active users. Live Twitter interviews are done using a hashtag which is attached to all the tweets. It's useful to use a tool like TweetChat.com or another monitoring application during the interview. These tools will automatically add the hashtag to the end of every tweet and make it easier to follow as the whole interview will show up on the one page without the clutter of the Twitter newsfeed.

- **Google+ hangouts**. Google+ now has 359 million monthly active users. The hangouts are one of the best and most popular features on the site. Filming yourself with your webcam you can do a live video interview, panel discussion, book reading or other event. By live streaming your hangout to your YouTube channel you can then easily share the content on your other social media sites and even embed it on your blog or website.

Video Chats. These are often done via skype or by using an online meeting software like https://www.meetingburner.com/.

Blog posts.

- Interviews

- Guest posts

- Spotlight features

- Reviews

Virtual Book Signings. These can easily be done using a site like authorgraph.com. If you can set up a webcam to film your computer screen as you write out the autographs you can live feed the event by combining it with a Google+ hangout for extra impact.

Webinars. Presentations are a great way to establish yourself as an expert in your field and build your author brand.

Radio interviews and readings. Blog Talk Radio is probably the most well known but there are many other internet radio stations on the web. There are literally thousands of internet radio programs that broadcast from these sites and plenty that love to have guests call in for interviews or to talk about certain topics.

Just because you're touring your book doesn't mean it has to be a solo affair. Ask other authors in your niche to join you for group interviews and panel discussions. Not only will this give you a larger reach, as each participant will promote the event, but you'll also be able to offer your audience more varied content whilst at the same time still promoting your book.

Section 2: How to Organise Your Own Tour

How to organise your own tour: Chapter 4

Your target audience

"The aim of marketing is to know and understand the customer so well the product or service fits him and sells itself."

Peter F. Drucker

Who is your target reader?

Probably one of the most important questions you should be asking yourself as a writer is "Who is your target reader". This is valid for both freelance writers and book authors.

Think about this for a minute; your favourite author isn't necessarily a better writer than all the others. They're your favourite because they write what you like and want to read.

During your virtual book tour, much like you did for your book, you need to recognize, acknowledge and write for your readers.

As much as you might want to believe that your master piece has a universal theme that will appeal to all ages of men, women and children from any where across the globe, you need to have a more specific answer to the question "who is your target audience?". "Everyone" just won't cut it.

Some writers have a target reader in mind when they start work on a piece and write every sentence with that audience in mind. Others just write and then have to identify their reader once they've finished.

Knowing your target reader will not only help get your work published. It's also an important element of your marketing campaign.

You've written a book and finally the big day has arrived. You are becoming a published author. You've decided to organise a virtual tour to help launch the book. Knowing your target audience will help you pick suitable websites, blogs, radio shows etc... to approach. Whilst a general book site is good, a site that specialises in your genre is better.

Define your target reader. Write a quick description of your ideal reader- Who would *love* your book?

Now think about the demographics of that person. What age range are they in? Geographic location? Where do they hang out? What activities do they do? Their hobbies? The more detailed description you can create of who your ideal reader is, the easier it will be to make sure you target sites that will reach them.

Here's an example of a quick ideal reader description by DT Linda Gross, Author of The Caveman Formula. (DT4M, Dating Tips for Men).

"My ideal readers are (in this order):
1. Male. 18-30. Just starting out, perhaps his parents
went thru a divorce and he wants to understand
women and skip unlearning bad habits.
2. Male. 31-50. Divorced, shy, player,
inactive/passive male. Has made tons of mistakes
with women and finally wants to be happy and have
an easier time with women.
3. Curious Women. Women who want to find out how
their actions affect men (to attract a better quality
man).

The highest concentration of my readers live in NYC
(even though I am a native Angeleno), followed by
major east coast cities, and in 3rd place would be Los
Angeles readers."

As you can see, this example breaks down the ideal readers for this book and offers a brief description of their age, social status, character, motivation, and touches on the geographic location too.

On reading this description it's clear that looking for sites geared towards advice about relationships, particularly those based in the NYC area, would be a good starting point in finding stops that will reach the target audience for this book.

Virtual Book Tours

By having a specific target audience, and finding stops for your virtual book tour that reach that audience, you greatly increase your chances of success.

How to organise your own tour: Chapter 5

How to find stops

"All successful people men and women are big dreamers. They imagine what their future could be, ideal in every respect, and then they work every day toward their distant vision, that goal or purpose."

Brian Tracy

How to find stops

Now you've worked out who your target audience is you need to find tour stops that will expose you to that audience. In this chapter I'll take you through a few methods for finding stops for your virtual book tour.

So how do you find people to host you on your tour and help you promote your book?

Ask

Sometimes it's easy to over look the most obvious solutions. If you already have people in your network that have sites suited to your target audience ask them if they would host you as part of your virtual book tour. As you already know each other there is a high possibility that they will say yes.

You can also take asking to another level and post a sign up form on the landing page for your book. This can easily be done using a form in Google Drive.

During September and October I'll be touring the web to promote the launch of the book. To sign up to host me during the virtual book tour for it's release please fill out the quick form below.

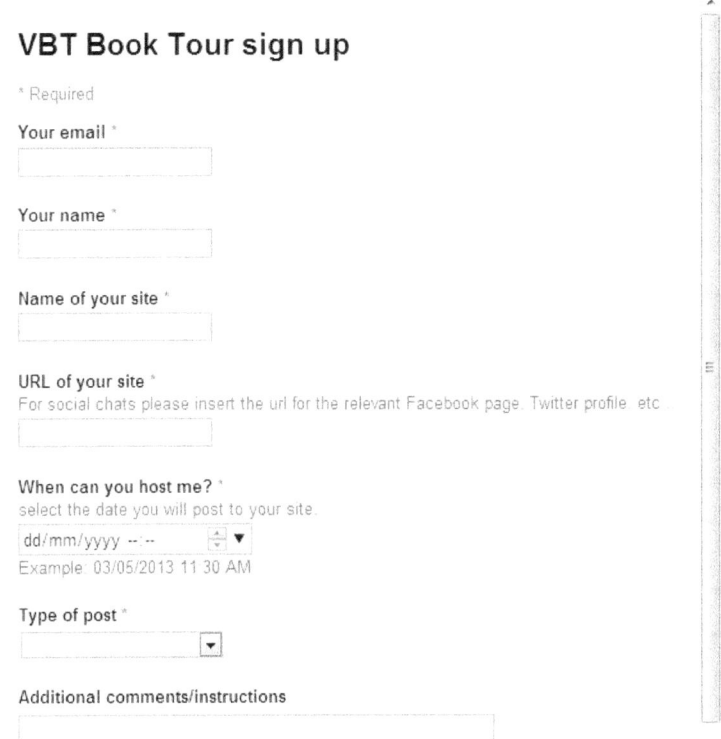

Example of the sign up form I used for this book

Use your social media profiles

Don't under estimate the power of social media. If you have a fan page on Facebook (which I hope you do) the people that follow your page are already interested in what you do. Use this to your advantage and optimise your page to encourage your fans to host you during your virtual book tour.

Create a banner for your page that highlights your book and announces your upcoming tour. Include a call-to-action inviting people to join your tour. Once you've uploaded the banner it will show up on the newsfeed just like any other images you post to your page. This is why you should fill out the description with information about your tour and a link to your sign up page on your website.

Example of the banner I used for this book

When people click on the banner they get taken to the photo page which includes some information about the tour and the link to the sign up page on my website.

This is what people see when they click the banner

You might also consider creating a tab for your page where people can sign up to be part of your tour. Alternatively pin a post to the top of your page.

I've used Facebook as the example here but this strategy can be adopted for most social media platforms.

If you use YouTube create a video telling viewers about your upcoming release and asking them if they would like to host you. Again here you'll want to optimise the description area to include information about the book, the tour, and the link to your sign up page.

If you use Twitter create a tweet campaign to encourage sign ups. As Twitter is such a high traffic site you might want to consider using different methods of posting. You can easily cross promote by sharing your video's from YouTube. Post a banner with the link to your sign up page or just use plain text. And don't forget to ask your followers to retweet your posts. Tweets that specifically ask followers to "Retweet" or "RT" receive 12 times retweet rates than those who don't use this call-to-action.

Directories

There are numerous directories online that list blogs by category. One example is The Book Blogger Directory. For a good list of blog directories check out the RSS Top 55. This site is basically a directory of blog directories. You'll be sure to find some interesting sites here what ever your genre!

Search

Then of course there are search engines like www.Google.com that will give you a wide variety of sites suitable for your target audience when you insert the right request.

In this example I did a search for sites that accept guest posts, specifying Romance books. As you can see it called up 427,000 results.

How To Find Stops

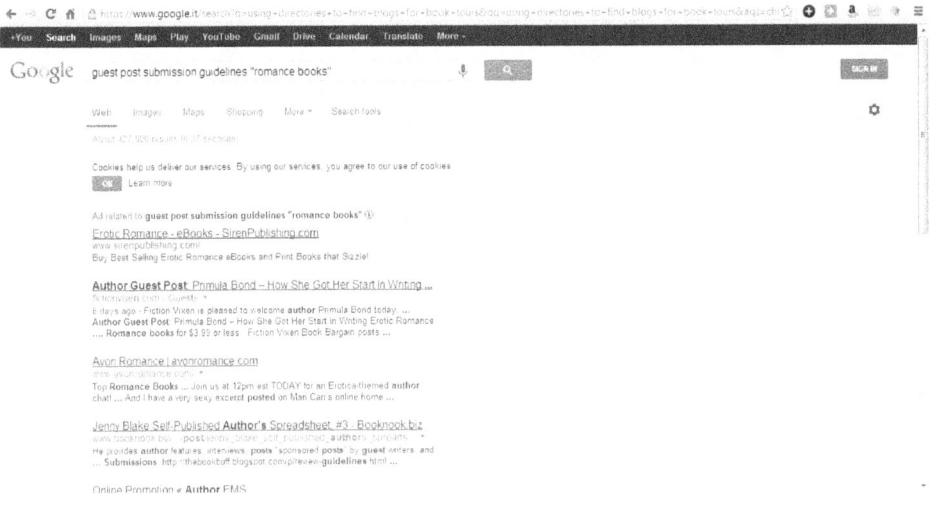

In this example I searched for sites that interview authors, specifying non-fiction books and it pulled up 3,540,000 results.

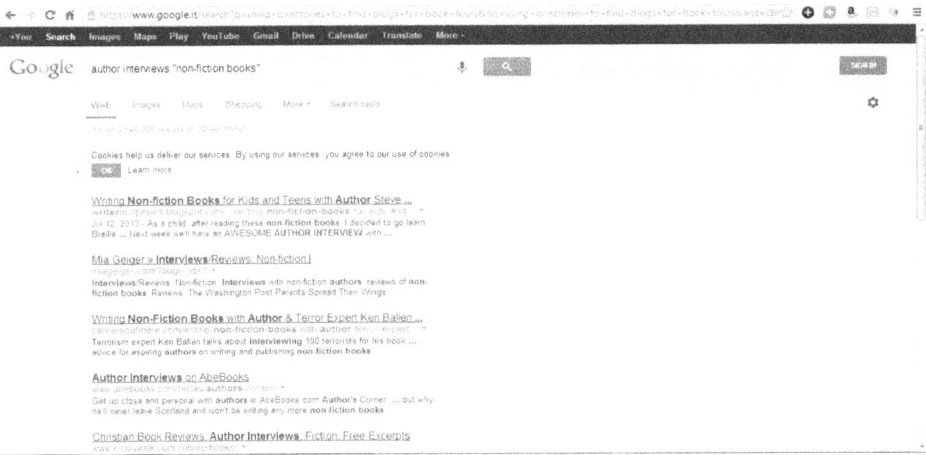

By doing a search for sites in your specific genre you can also see which sites show up best in the results. Being featured on these sites will get you good exposure.

Host sites

The web is full of sites and resources that serve as a database of potential hosts. Check out sites like My Blog Guest and sign up for updates from HARO (Help a Reporter) and Radio Guest List. These sites can be a great way to find opportunities to be hosted and are all completely free.

How to organise your own tour: Chapter 6

Being a good guest

"Success in this industry is not in finding the right person, but in becoming the right person."

Dr. Forrest Shaklee

How to be a good guest

A Virtual Book Tour needs hosts. Without stops you wouldn't have a tour and as most of the people that will be hosting you on your tour will be doing so completely free of charge it's important that you show them your gratitude by being a good guest.

Your hosts are offering you valuable support and helping you spread the word about your book. Make sure you make it worth their while.

Creating a good impression is important. Even more so if you plan to promote future books as depending on your actions during your tour the host will decide whether they would want you back again in the future or not.

I run several blogs and like most bloggers I take notice of good guests and the bad ones. I'll always find space to host a guest that leaves a good impression. Things like following the submission guidelines, promoting the post, replying to comments and simply saying thank you can really help make you stand out as a good guest.

Those that mess me around, don't take the time to reply to comments or fail to do their bit to promote their post generally don't get hosted again.

Here's a few tips on how to be a good guest blogger:

- **Follow their submission guidelines.** A lot of bloggers post submission guidelines to their site in order to make their life easier. They want to receive the content in the format that works best for them so if they offer guidelines follow them to the letter.

- **Send them all the information they could need.** It's a good idea to send your media kit along with a professional looking author photo and your books cover art when you submit your content (unless stated in the guidelines not to). This way you look organised and professional and your host has all the information they might need for the post all in the one place. Trust me, there is nothing more annoying than having to waste time searching through emails to find content. Bloggers like it when you make life easy for them. I'll cover media kits in chapter 9 along with other promotional materials for your tour.

- **Read the blog, leave some comments and share some of their recent posts.** They are helping you by hosting you on their site. It's good ethics to help them too by driving traffic to their site. By sharing some of their posts with your audience prior to being hosting on their site you also increase the chances of your readers seeing and engaging with your post as they will be familiar with both you and the site.

- **Research the blog and submit a post that is well suited to the site and it's readers.** By reading their site you'll have a better idea of the sort of content that their readers enjoy. Check what content gets the most comments, shares and likes. You'll also be able to make sure you offer them something new.

- **Supply them with content their site is missing.** Whilst you need to make sure your post is in keeping with the topic niche of the hosts site, you also want to try and give them something new. Use your own unique experience and skills to fill the needs of the host and their readers.

- **Make the job of the host as easy as possible.** If they have guidelines, follow them to the letter. Supply them with appropriate images to use with the post and any other additional information they might want to use.

- **Be reliable.** If you promise to send your content by a certain date, send it by that date. Don't leave your host and their readers hanging. Not only is this unprofessional, it will also damage your reputation.

- **Promote your post.** Don't just write the guest post and leave it to the host to promote it. It's part of the deal as a guest blogger that you help bring readers to the site. Share the link to your post everywhere you can to drive as much traffic as possible.

- **Reply to comments.** Part of the reason for guest blogging is to connect with new readers. If someone takes the time to leave a comment on your post, make sure you reply to them. Even if it's just to thank them for their input.

- **Give thanks.** Thank the host publicly by leaving a comment on the post. Thank them again by email and/or via their social media pages. If they have accounts with applications like branchout write them a testimonial to thank them. And then thank them again!

Bottom-line: Be the sort of guest you'd like to have visit your own site.

Getting the most out of each stop

"Connect, create meaning, make a difference, matter, be missed"

Seth Godin

Maximising the impact of your stops

As I just covered in Chapter 6, you need to do more than just send off some content to your hosts. In order to get the most out of each stop you need to make sure you engage with the host and readers and pull your weigh in the promotion of the post too. In this chapter I'll take you through a few strategies for getting the most out of each stop.

Promote the stop

Whilst the host will probably be promoting the post to drive traffic to the site you too need to help spread the word. Make sure you share the link to your post via your social media sites and encourage your followers to drop by to read your post and leave a comment. Ask them to share the post too. As I mentioned before sometimes all you need to do is ask.

The more people that know about your post, the higher your chances of people stopping to read it, interact via comments, and share it with others. Your chances of converting readers into sales also increases as the more people that find out about your book the greater the probability that some will buy it so; Like it, Tweet it, Share it, Digg it, Pin it, and blog about it. You might even want to film a video for YouTube telling people about it. If you have a newsletter, mention the stop and invite your subscribers to come on over and check it out.

Interact with the readers

Having the chance to chat with readers, answer their questions and listen to their feedback is priceless. Even those that just leave a comment to say "good luck" or "congrats on your new release" have taken the time to show their support. Make sure you thank them and invite them to connect with you further via your social media profiles. The fact that they took the time to leave a comment, however small and simple, shows they have an interest in you and/or your book. This is your chance to start building a relationship with them and turn them into fans.

Think long term

Although you'll be putting most of your energy into promoting your post during your virtual book tour it doesn't need to stop there. Continue to share the post and encourage interactions weeks or even months after the posting date.

One of the huge benefits of a virtual book tour is that once the content is posted, in most cases, it's online for good. Unlike an in person event that lasts just one day, a blog post will be available days, weeks, months and even years later.

Quote your post

Use the content of your stop in new content you create. If you do a Google+ hangout where you're interviewed about your book use it as a reference for a future blog post with a link back to the tour post and get some extra mileage out of it.

For example:

In an interview for an internet radio show when the host asks about your thoughts on self publishing give a summary and then mention that you recently wrote a guest post on the subject for a blog during your virtual book tour and let listeners know where they can find the post.

How to organise your own tour: Chapter 8

The tour schedule

"Don't build links. Build relationships"

Rand Fishkin

Your tour schedule

Your tour schedule is your calendar of tour stops. It includes information like; the date of the stop, the url, host name, site name and the type of post you're being hosted for.

Fans will often follow all your tour stops so it's a good idea to post your tour schedule to your website, blog, newsletter and social media profiles.

You might also want to consider creating a linky to add to each tour stop.

What is a Linky?

A Linky is a clickable list of links.

To make it easy for people to follow your tour from one stop to the next it's a good idea to create a Linky with the whole tour schedule. You can then send the embed code for the Linky to each of your hosts to be included at the end of your post.

Note: Not all hosts will want to include the Linky but giving them the option never hurts.

There are several tools available online that allow you to build a linky free of charge. Some worth checking out are http://www.linkytools.com/ and http://www.simply-linked.com/. Both are popular, easy to use, and completely free.

Now let's take a closer look at a tour schedule and what kind of information you might want to include.

For your personal tour schedule/plan:

Having a tour schedule is essential to carrying out a successful tour as it will help you stay organising and keep all the important details in the one place.

- **Name of your host.** This is important because you should be able to address each host by name. Doing a virtual book tour is a great opportunity to build relationships with readers but also to grow your support network. Hosts are valuable to your marketing efforts, and as I mentioned before, you wouldn't have much of a tour without them.

- **Name of the host site.** In some cases you'll be hosted on a personal site that uses the name of the host whereas on other occasions the site will have a business name.

- **URL of host site.** A clickable link to where you'll be hosted. This makes it quick and easy to reference the site when creating your content for the stop.

- **Email of host.** You'll need to contact your host to set up the tour stop, send them your content and any other information they might need, follow up that everything is set for your post, and to thank them for hosting you.

- **Date hosting.** Along with the date you should also include the time for any live events. Make sure you've checked for time differences.

- **Type of post.** Note the type of post you're being hosted for e.g. guest post, interview, book feature, etc...

- **Guidelines.** Here you'll make a note of any submission guidelines and other information regarding your stop e.g. if it's a guest post make a note of the topic, length, and any other specifics required. If it's a radio interview include the call in number.

- **Content sent.** Make a note of when you send the content to the host.

- **Stop confirmed.** Here you'll make a note when you receive confirmation from the host that your post has been programmed for publishing. In the case of live events you should follow up the day before to make sure everything is ready.

- **Feedback.** This is where you'll summarise how the spot went. Did the host post as planned? What reaction did the stop get? If possible include some statistics like the number of page views to your post, number of comments, shares, etc... This information will be useful when planning future tours.

For your public tour schedule:

- **When you'll be hosted.** Include the date (and time if it's a live event like a Facebook Wall Chat or radio interview).

- **Where you'll be hosted.** Include the direct link to your post as and when possible. This way people will be able to automatically find your post without having the search the host site for it

- **Type of post.** Let followers know what type of stop it is. Interview, guest post about..., book feature, etc...

-

Section 3:
Promoting a Tour

Promoting a Tour:
Chapter 9

Promotional Materials for the Tour

"Create something people want to share"

John Jantsch

Promotional materials

Promoting a virtual book tour is easier when you have the right materials to hand. In this chapter I'll take you through some of the promotional materials you can use when organising a virtual book tour.

Media Kit

This is a must for any virtual book tour. It contains all the information anyone could need about you and your book. What to include in your media kit:

- Your book cover art

- Your book details; Publisher, release date, ISBN/ASIN, number of pages, etc...

- Your book purchasing links

- Your book description

- A press release announcing the launch of the book/ your virtual book tour.

- Your website url

- Your blog url

- Your other social media links

- Your author bio

- Your author photo

- A sample interview

- Reviews of book

- Click to tweets and pre-written social media status updates for easy sharing.

Press releases

Press releases have been used to announce events for years and are still a powerful marketing method. When writing a press release to announce your virtual book tour it's a good idea to start with a brief summary of what a virtual book tour is as some people may not be familiar with the process.

Your press release is the "who", "what", "why", "how", and "when" of your virtual book tour.

My cyber friend Jennifer Mattern has an excellent press release template available on her website All Freelance Writing that can be downloaded free of charge.

FOR IMMEDIATE RELEASE

Your Press Release Heading / Title Here (remember: catchy, not cutesy!)

Write a two to four sentence summary of your news angle here. While a summary can be used in either online or offline press release distribution, if you're distributing the release offline (such as via fax), you can substitute the summary for a one-line sub-heading.

City, State – Date – The body of your press release starts here, on the same line as your dateline (the location and date). The first paragraph of your press release body should briefly answer the questions of who, what, when, where, and why.

You can use the next body paragraph of the book launch press release to expand upon the "why" aspect of the news angle (why your book is timely or relevant, or why people should care about its launch), or you can use this area to simply provide further details.

Somewhere in the body of the press release, it's a good idea to have a quote from someone involved. Do *not* make the quote a testimonial. That's advertising; not publicity, and it can have a release rejected from distribution sites online or ignored by journalists who get their hands on it.

Add any remaining details to the end of your book launch press release body, such as information about where the book is being distributed, its retail price, etc (background info that's not vital to the launch news aspect).

About the Author (use your name instead of "the author" for the boilerplate lead-in)

Include a paragraph after the press release body as a short author bio. This is where you'll mention your own qualifications to write the book in more detail (adding too much to the press release body paragraphs can take away from the news value unless something in your credentials is incredibly newsworthy or timely in itself). A boilerplate often remains the same, or very similar, from one press release about your book to another.

For more information about BOOK TITLE, please visit BOOK WEBSITE or contact PUBLICIST'S NAME at PHONE NUMBER. (I'd always suggest a phone number here over an email address, because it's simply more professional and can make it easier to get interviews set up – this area of the release is called the "call to action.)

(Use this symbol or -30- to signify the end of a press release. While the general rule is to keep a news release to one page, if it does go onto a second page, use -more- on the bottom of the first page).

If you have addenda included with the release (book cover image, author photo, etc.), you can mention that after your call to action.

Here's the direct link for the template: http://allfreelancewriting.com/writers-resource-sample-press-release-template-for-a-book-launch/. You'll want to check out the other content on site while you're there too as it's packed full of useful tips and advice.

A landing page

A landing page is a single webpage with the goal of turning visitors into sales. It usually displays direct sales copy and strong calls to action. A good landing page will be targeted to a particular stream of traffic. The visitors are directed to this page after clicking on an online advertisement, email link, social media post with link, blog post with link, etc...

The landing page should be designed to prompt visitors into completing your desired action. In the case of a virtual book tour you want to use your landing page to get people to participate in your tour. You'll want a separate page to get them to buy copies of your book. Remember the goal of your landing page is to get visitors to do something specific. Don't confuse them with too many calls to action. It's better to set up separate landing pages for each task you want them to perform e.g. "sign up for tour", "buy the book", etc...

Here's a few tips for creating a landing page that converts:

- **Limit navigation.** You want visitors to the page to concentrate on your calls to action. Don't distract them with too many links. Hide your site navigation bar and focus on what you want them to do. e.g. sign up to be part of your virtual book tour.

- **Enable sharing.** Make it easy for people to share your landing page by adding social share buttons to your page.

- **Keep copy brief.** Make sure everything on the page is relevant to it's purpose.

- **Keep forms short.** Only ask for essential information in your form. Don't risk turning people off by asking too many questions. As long as you get their email address you can always follow up later if needed.

- **List the benefits of your book.** Break your text into easy to scan bullet points for quick reading. Describe your book from the readers point of view e.g. how the book will help them.

- **List the benefits of taking part in the tour.** Give them a reason to participate. What's in it for them?

- **Use visual cues**. Use visuals to keep the focus on the important features of the page e.g. getting them to take part in your virtual book tour. Use arrows and images to draw their attention to your call to action.

- **Use video.** If you feel comfortable on film, video is a great way to create a big impact in a small space. It allows visitors to get to know you better, let's you include more information, and reinforce your call to action (getting them to sign up to host you during your virtual book tour).

To summarize; keep it simple, compelling, and include one clear call to action.

Graphics

Visual content catches the eye. The right graphics can do wonders to strengthen your promotional efforts for your virtual book tour.

Here's a few examples of useful graphics you might want to consider using during your virtual book tour:

- **A tour banner.** A simple banner that shows your book cover and your author photo (a clear, professional headshot). It should also list your book title, tour dates, and a link to your website.

- **Social media banners.** Each social media site allows you to upload a cover banner.

Facebook

Cover banner 815 px X 315 px

When uploading a cover banner to your Facebook page make sure you fill out the description section and include a link to your landing page.

If you choose to create a tab for your tour the size for the tab image that shows at the top of your page is 111 px X 74 px.

Twitter

Header banner 520 px X 260 px

Google+

Cover banner 2120 px X 1192 px

- **Social media post images.** Each social media site has different sizing for the pictures you upload to your profile. By using the right sized image you can draw more attention on your profile and in the newsfeeds. Here's a list of the current best sizing for images on the top sites:

Facebook

Timeline image preview 403 px X 403 px

Highlight post/Milestone image 843 px X 403 px

Newsfeed shared image (here you have 3 choices)

398 px X 296 px

320 px X 320 px

296 px X 398 px

Twitter

Recent images 90 px X 90 px

Shared image 375 px X 375 px

Google+

Shared image 497 px X 373 px

- **Promotional graphics for interviews, etc...** For these you'll want to include important information like the date and time of the event, clearly state where the event will take place, and maybe add a brief description of what will be covered. Include your author photo for author branding.

  You can easily make simple graphics using free graphics programs like Microsoft Paint. I personally use Adobe Illustrator to create mine but there are many other programs out there that are easy to use

  .

How to Promote a Tour

"No one ever succeeds without the help of others"

Jay Abraham

Promoting your tour

In this chapter I'm going to take you through ways to promote your virtual book tour and attract tour followers. You'll learn about pre-tour build up, setting up a webpage for your tour, creating event pages, utilizing social media, organizing give-aways and more.

Pre-tour build up

In order to make your tour as successful as possible people need to know about it. You need to spread the word about your upcoming tour and get people excited about it. You want as many people as possible to know about your tour. A few ways you can do this include:

- Create a tour banner and post it everywhere with a link back to your books landing page.

- Spread the word through your social media profiles. Let your friends know you have a virtual book tour coming up and encourage them to take part.

- Create a hashtag (# symbol followed by your keyword) for your tour and announce your upcoming tour letting people know they will be able to follow it using that hashtag (you'll use the hashtag during your tour on posts too).

- Create banners for your social media profiles that promote the tour.

- Record and share some video's letting viewers know about your upcoming tour and why they should be part of it.

- Post behind the scenes content of you preparing for the tour. Photo's of you working on guest posts or interviews, how to video's showing what you're doing to prepare for your virtual book tour, or status updates letting your readers know what your doing (with a picture of the books cover art attached).

Create a webpage for your tour

I covered landing pages in chapter 9 so I won't go into that here. Instead I'll concentrate on setting up a webpage for your tour.

It's a good idea to create a webpage for your virtual book tour. This page should include all the information anyone could possibly want to know about the tour, you and your book.

Include:

- your tour schedule

- your book cover art

- your book blurb

- your book details e.g. ISBN, number of pages, etc...

- purchasing links

- review comments

- your tour banner

- links to event pages (I'll get to those in a minute)

- call to action buttons e.g. add to Goodreads button

- your video book trailer

- link to your media kit

- link to your press releases

Event pages

Create event pages for your virtual book tour on your website and social media sites. By creating an event for your tour you increase awareness and give people more options of how to follow and participate in your tour.

Once you've set up your event page invite your connections to join the event. Update the event page each day. Some ideas for content to post include; links to your tour stops, showcase your hosts, run a give away, post behind the scenes video's or exclusive material just for those joining the tour. And most importantly thank your supporters.

Give-aways

Give-aways can be a great way of getting people to take action and raise awareness of your book.

Give away copies of your book

Use sites where avid readers gather like Goodreads.com to set up a book give away. The people that use these sites are often on the look out for new books and are the sort of people that post reviews of the books they read.

You might also want to consider setting up a book give away via your website, social media profile, or newsletter as a reward to your fans for their support.

Widgets

Tools like Rafflecopter.com make setting up a give away easy. You just insert what people need to do to enter the give away (e.g. like your Facebook page, follow you on Twitter or blog about your book), and set the dates. Rafflecopter will automatically pick the winners for you at the end of the give away.

It also makes it easy to promote the give away as they give you the html code so you can embed the give away widget on your website or blog. This means you can also include it in your media kit and make it available for your tour hosts to include in your post when they host you.

Special offers and discounts

Another way to help promote your tour is to set up special offers or discounts to run during your tour period. If your book is normally priced at 5.99 set the price to 1.99 for the duration of your tour as a limited time offer.

Another option is to create a discount code that can be used when purchasing your book. These can easily be done if you self publishing through Createspace and work nicely with a virtual book tour as you can include the discount code in your tour stops as a thank you to the people who follow your tour.

Post-Tour

"Marketing is not an event, but a process . . . It has a beginning, a middle, but never an end, for it is a process. You improve it, perfect it, change it, even pause it. But you never stop it completely."

Jay Conrad Levinson

When the tour is over

Your virtual book tour is over. Hopefully you'll have reached the goals you set for your tour and be rejoicing in the buzz you've created for your book. All of this is fantastic and well deserved as by now you'll have realized that organizing a successful virtual book tour takes time and effort. This isn't the moment to sit back and relax though.

Although the official dates of your tour have passed your work is not over. With your virtual book tour you started the snow ball effect but you need to keep it rolling.

What you need to do post-tour:

- **Give thanks.** Thank your hosts both publically via your blog and social media channels and privately by sending them a personalized email that acknowledges how much you appreciate their support. Also thank everyone that followed your tour, bought your book, left reviews, and helped spread the word.

- **Share tour posts.** Continue to share your tour stops by sharing them via your social media channels. One of the best things about doing a virtual book tour is that the content you create is still available long after the tour is over.

- **Repurpose content.** During your virtual book tour you created content. That content can be reformatted and turned into new content e.g. If you did a Google hangout during your tour write up the transcript and use it for a blog post. If you did a radio interview create a video using the audio from the interview. If you did a guest post take the key points of the article and make an infographic. By repurposing your content you get more mileage out of it.

- **Check your metrics**

You'll want to measure the success of your efforts by checking your metrics. You'll have already noted your rankings pre-tour and will probably have checked them again during the tour. Check them again now to see the impact your tour has had on sales, number of new followers, etc...

Section 4: Useful Resources

Useful Resources:
Chapter 12

Host sites

"Understand that you need to sell you and your ideas in order to advance your career, gain more respect, and increase you success, influence and income."

Jay Abraham

Sites that host

In this chapter you'll find a list of sites that host people for interviews, guest posts and book features. Some are general book related sites whilst other are targeted towards specific genres.

http://WritersAndAuthors.blogspot.com

http://digitalbooktoday.com/5-dbt-author-interview/

http://www.authorspromotingauthors.org/p/contactour-features.html

Virtual Book Tours

http://lucianbarnes.blogspot.com

http://readindies.blogspot.it/p/get-featured.html

http://allthingswriting.blogspot.it/p/guest-bloggers-wanted.html

http://terri-forehand.blogspot.com

http://virginialorijennings.com/blog

http://wordstomouth.com/authors/

http://www.whohub.com/en/

http://doctorsnotes-shy.blogspot.it/

http://foreverbklover.blogspot.it/

http://www.proactivereport.com

Host Sites

http://www.mediabistro.com/galleycat

http://www.girlintehlockerroom.blogspot.com

http://www.storms.typepad.com

http://www.Buzzmachine.com

http://www.blogcritics.org/books

http://www.kimbofo.typepad.com/readingmatters

http://www.moonishgirl.com

http://www.bookfetish.org

http://www.booksquare.com

http://www.bookslut.com

Virtual Book Tours

http://www.bookninja.com

http://www.litlove.wordpress.com

http://www.lbc.typepad.com

http://www.bookdwarf.com

http://www.inspirationforum.co.uk/index.php

http://www.jenniferwrightauthor.com/index.html

http://siefkenpublications.blogspot.com

http://afstewartblog.blogspot.com/

http://www.amymilesbooks.blogspot.com/

http://www.muttonline.com

http://www.indiesunlimited.com

Host Sites

http://www.wonderfulreadofthemonth.blogspot.com/

http://teddygross.blogspot.it

http://www.jonpbloch.com/interviews.html

http://sylviabrowder.com/

http://paperdragonink.com

http://kriswampler.wordpress.com

http://morgenbailey.wordpress.com/blog-interviews/

http://www.thoughtfulreflections.blogspot.com

http://writersoldier.blgospot.com

http://sostacythought.wordpress.com

Virtual Book Tours

http://childrensandteenbookconnection.wordpress.com

http://www.vrleavitt.com

http://carolmarlenesmith.blogspot.com

http://barbaraehrentreu.blogspot.com

Useful Resources:
Chapter 13

Internet radio, podcasts and web TV

"If you do build a great experience, customer tell each other about that. Word of mouth is very powerful."

Jeff Bezos

Talk to the host

In this chapter I've listed internet radio shows, podcasts and web TV shows that host authors for discussions, interviews, and book readings.

http://tothnews.libsyn.com/

http://achieveradio.com/

http://www.wnbnetworkwest.com/WnbAuthorsShow.html

Virtual Book Tours

http://www.TalkStoryTV.com

http://www.blogtalkradio.com/bgr

http://www.blogtalkradio.com/soundauthors

http://www.blogtalkradio.com/christianauthorsontour

http://www.blogtalkradio.com/thebeyond

http://www.blogtalkradio.com/kims

http://www.blogtalkradio.com/insidelenz

http://www.blogtalkradio.com/compulsivereader

http://www.blogtalkradio.com/librarylovefest

http://www.blogtalkradio.com/book-club-girl

Other Hosts

http://www.blogtalkradio.com/romanceradio

http://www.blogtalkradio.com/topshelf

http://www.blogtalkradio.com/authorsread

http://www.blogtalkradio.com/soundauthors

http://www.blogtalkradio.com/urbanliteraryreview

http://www.blogtalkradio.com/chicksonlit

http://www.blogtalkradio.com/asa-blog-talk

http://www.blogtalkradio.com/writers-radio-show

http://www.blogtalkradio.com/writerslifechats

http://www.nhptv.org/authors

Virtual Book Tours

http://www.thedailyshow.com/guests

http://www.booktv.org/

http://www.wiredforbooks.org/swaim/

http://blip.tv/the-indie-media-show

http://readingandwritingpodcast.com/

http://www.learnoutloud.com/Podcast-Directory/Literature

Useful Resources:
Chapter 14

Book reviewers

"Nothing influences people more than a recommendation from a trusted friend."

Mark Zuckerberg

Get readers sharing

In this chapter I've listed sites that regularly post book reviews. You might also want to contact the Top Reviewers on Amazon for your genre.

http://reviewingshelf.wordpress.com/

http://scarletsilhouettes.blogspot.it/

http://book-spark.blogspot.it/

http://randiesreviews.blogspot.it/

Virtual Book Tours

http://www.reviewbuzzz.blogspot.in/

http://bookstomorrow.blogspot.it/p/contact-us.html

http://www.indtale.com/submit-book-review

http://www.armchairinterviews.com/submit-a-book-for-review.aspx

http://bookbag.areavoices.com/

http://katebrauning.wordpress.com/

http://readingforsanity.blogspot.it/

http://booksandpals.blogspot.it/

http://candysraves.com/

http://www.indieheart.com/

Book Reviewers

http://www.undergroundbookreviews.com/index.html

http://achaury.blogspot.it/

http://chaptersthree.blogspot.it/

http://ginger-read.blogspot.it/

http://thepaperbackpursuer.blogspot.it/

http://www.thebrainybookblog.com/

http://textsandteas.tumblr.com/

http://thebookhookup.com/

http://indieauthorbookreviews.wordpress.com/

http://thebusybibliophile.com/

http://c9creviews.com/

http://www.indiesentreader.com/

http://www.booksforcompany.com/

http://www.rtbookreviews.com/

http://heartfeltwords4kids.blogspot.com

http://myheartbelongs2books.blogspot.com

http://thenewbookreview.blogspot.com

Useful Resources: Chapter 15

Sites that promote free days and special offers

"Give them quality. That's the best kind of advertising."

Milton Hershey

Promotions and special offers

In this chapter I've listed sites that help you promote your free download days, discounts, and special offers.

http://ebookdailydeals.com/

http://ebooks.addall.com/amazonfree.html

http://www.atozwire.com/

http://bargainebookhunter.com/category/free/

http://blog.booksontheknob.org/

http://www.dailycheapreads.com/category/free

http://junior.dailycheapreads.com/category/free

http://www.dailyfreebooks.com/

http://www.daily-free-ebooks.com/category/free-kindle-books/

http://danstoolshed.com/?cat=9

http://ebookshabit.com/

http://www.theereadercafe.com/

http://www.freereadfeed.com

http://ereadernewstoday.com/category/free-kindle-books/

Promotion Sites

http://www.ereaderperks.com/

http://fkb.me/

http://www.freebookdude.com/p/list-your-free-book.html

http://www.freebookshub.com/books/free-kindle-books/

http://freebooksy.com/

http://www.freeebooksdaily.com/

http://www.fkbooksandtips.com/

http://freekindleebooks.com/

http://freesci-fi.com/

http://www.freestufftimes.com/?s=kindle

http://www.gospelebooks.net/free-christian-ebooks/

http://hundredzeros.com/

http://hunt4freebies.com/free-magazines/kindle-ebooks/

http://www.icravefreebies.com/category/free-books-guides/

http://www.iloveebooks.com/

http://ireaderreview.com/category/free-books/

http://kindleclassics.blogspot.it/

http://kindle-free.com/

http://kindlenationdaily.com/knd-free-book-search-tool/

http://us.kinlib.com/130809A/

Promotion Sites

http://www.mybookandmycoffee.com/search/label/Free%20eBooks

http://www.new-daily-free-ebooks.com/

http://www.notwiddletwaddle.com/

http://onehundredfreebooks.com/

http://www.pixelofink.com/category/free-kindle-books/

http://the-cheap.net/category/freebies/

http://www.wlfreebook.com/

http://www.worldliterarycafe.com/forum/171

http://www.yourdailyebooks.com/category/free-kindle-books/

Virtual Book Tours

http://better-book.blogspot.it/

https://www.facebook.com/FreeEbooksDownloads

Useful Resources:
Chapter 16

Sites for submitting press releases

"Make it about them, not about you."

Simon Sinek

Read all about it!

In this chapter I've listed websites that allow you to submit your press releases. Most of them are completely free to use.

http://www.openpr.com

http://newswiretoday.com/

http://www.przoom.com/

http://www.onlineprnews.com

http://www.1888pressrelease.com/

http://addpr.com/

http://bignews.biz/

http://www.free-press-release.com/

http://www.i-newswire.com/

http://www.ignitepoint.com/

http://www.netforcepr.com/

http://www.newsinsites.com/

http://www.newsactive.net/

http://www.clickpress.com/releases/index.shtml

Sites For Press Releases

http://www.24-7pressrelease.com

Final thoughts

Final thoughts

Conclusion

"The way to get started is to quit talking and begin doing."

Walt Disney

Time to tour!

Now it's time to put all the information in this book into action. In this book I've laid out the how to and step by step of organising a virtual book tour. You are now prepared to organise your own virtual book tour. As I've covered a lot of information over the duration of this book I thought it would be a good idea to summarise the main points here into a step by step check list for organizing a virtual book tour.

1. Set your goals for the tour

2. Work out your strengths and weaknesses and identify the types of content to include

3. Identify your target audience

4. Create landing page

5. Start pre-tour build up

6. Find tour stops

7. Create media kit and other promotional materials

8. Write press releases and submit to sites

9. Publish tour schedule and promote

10. Create content for tour stops and send to hosts

11. Check your metrics (pre-tour)

12. Promote tour stops

13. Contact every person who has helped with and supported the virtual book tour and thank them for their support

14. Repurpose tour content

15. Check your metrics (post-tour) to see what worked

This book is designed to give you all the information you need to be able to organizing and carry out your own virtual book tour. As with all marketing efforts the results will be different for each person and book. With this book I hope to have given you a step by step process of what you can do and how to do it, and supplied you with some ideas to get you started.

Conclusion

Now I'm going to share with you the number 1 secret for virtual book tour success... the secret of a successful virtual book tour is YOU. You are the one that makes or breaks it. Your personality, talent, and skills will impact the success of your tour as will the quality of your content and your ability to engage people in your tour.

"You can do what you have to do, and sometimes you can do it even better than you think you can."

Jimmy Carter

Conclusion

Help spread the word!

"There is no exercise better for the heart than reaching down and lifting people up."

John Holmes

Share your thoughts

Thank you for reading this book. I hope you've found it useful and encourage you to leave a review on Amazon, Goodreads and any other site where reviews are posted. I really appreciate your help!

I also encourage you to share about this book on your social media channels.

Thank you so much for your help and I hope you enjoyed this book.

Jo Linsdell

Acknowledgements

Acknowledgments

Thanks to...

I'd just like to take a moment to thank the people that helped make this book possible.

Thanks to Guy Kawasaki for supplying the awesome template I used to produce this book as a bonus to his book *APE: Author, Publisher, Entrepreneur-How to Publish a Book* (I highly recommend checking out this book).

Thanks to my friend and author buddy Kathy Mashburn for helping out with editing and proofreading.

A big shout out to Virginia Jennings, who helped with the formatting of this print version and the rest of the gang in the *Where Writers and Author Meet* writers group that offered feedback and support during the writing of this book. I'm honored to be part of such a supportive and helpful group.

Thanks to my husband for listening to me talk about virtual book tours for months and still showing support all the way through.

And last but by no means least, thanks to my two wonderful children who let me write.

www.ingramcontent.com/pod-product-compliance
Lightning Source LLC
Chambersburg PA
CBHW070927290526
45795CB00001B/452